To our children and caregivers however you come to us, we love you and thank you.

Ranes
xxx

My love for you is everywhere
When you can't see me I still care
Sometimes you can see me and sometimes you can't
And when you can't see me, I live in your heart

I love you in the morning and
I love you all through the night and
If you're not too sure look around
You will see me in plain sight

If you miss me, there's no need to cry
Listen to your heart, I will sing you a lullaby
When I am not with you I am all around
In the park, in nature and in every sound

When the sun is in your warm embrace
That is me kissing you on your face
You are my world whether I am near or far
Look up in the sky and I am the star

When I see your favourite colour it makes me think of you
And when you see my favourite colour that's you thinking of me too
Close your eyes and open your heart when you don't think you're strong
And you will feel my love and strength from infinity and beyond

I will only leave you when you are ready for me to
And if you ask I will come back to you
It might not quite be the way that you see
But look all around you will see me

If I have gone off to work
It's because I want to look after you
So when you ask for a farm and a horse
I can say yes! Lets have two!

You are my ray of sunshine
You are my rainbow too
I love you I love you I love you so much
This you will see to be true

Sometimes we might be together
Sometimes we might be apart
Its ok because we are always together
When we live in each others heart

My love for you is forever
I thank you very much
For coming into my life
I love you oh so much

When I miss you and I want to cry
I keep you in my heart
I know that I can talk to you
And then we are not apart

And when I see you I will hug you and kiss you
I will love you and squeeze you too
You are the bestest person
And loving you is my favourite thing to do

Remember you are a genius
Remember you are a star
Remember that you are surrounded by love
Forever, wherever you are

CPSIA information can be obtained
at www.ICGtesting.com
Printed in the USA
BVHW020517261122
652779BV00016B/1156